D1135893

☺ LUSTRAL*

sertraline

INVICTA
PHARMACEUTICALS

A Division of Pfizer Limited

RICHBOROUGH
PHARMACEUTICALS

A Division of Pfizer Limited

Further information is available on request from: Pfizer Limited, Sandwich, Kent CT13 9NJ
*Trade mark

Patient Management Problems

in

Psychiatry

To Graeme McDonald

Patient Management Problems

in

Psychiatry

Questions and Answers

for

MRCPsych. Candidates

Paul H. McCrea F.D.S.R.C.S. Eng., M.R.C.Psych.

Senior Registrar

Northern Ireland Training Scheme in Psychiatry

and

Joanne D.E. Weir M.R.C.Psych.

Senior Registrar

Northern Ireland Training Scheme in Psychiatry

Rapid Communications of Oxford,
The Old Malthouse,
Paradise Street,
Oxford OX1 1LD, UK

©1993 Rapid Communications of Oxford, Ltd

ISBN
1 85650 003 9

A catalogue record for this title
is available from the British Library

The content of this book is the
work of the authors and does not
necessarily represent the view
of Invicta Pharmaceuticals or
its associated companies.

Set in Times 9.5pt on 10.5pt by Farrand Press on Prefis Book
Machine.
Printed by Information Press, Eynsham.

Foreword

In one sense examinations assess what examinations assess. Nevertheless, the Royal College of Psychiatrists, in seeking to establish high professional standards among trainees passing the Membership Examination, has implemented a comprehensive assessment of clinical competence. The thirty minute oral by two examiners is an important and rigorous feature of this process. While the College seeks to balance this rigour with fairness, factors outside their control ensure that candidates come to the viva with varying degrees of readiness, often through no fault of their own. Candidates training in academic centres and under the supervision of current or past examiners are often advantaged through better preparation for the examination experience.

While useful books are available to assist trainees with the written aspects of the Membership Examinations, there is a relative dearth of authoritative guidance for the Patient Management Oral. The present text therefore is a welcome addition to the examination armamentarium of trainees and a sterling effort by two trainees from the Northern Ireland Regional Training Scheme. Who better to advise than those who have sucessfully come through the experience. The efforts of two fellow trainees to make the path for those who follow them to the Membership Examination as fair and as clear as possible is to be commended. It is for the reader to judge how successful the authors have been in this enterprise. As an Examiner in several situations I can confidently recommend this book not only to trainees but to examiners and aspiring examiners, who must face the more daunting task of making a fair assessment of trainee clinical competence.

Roy McClelland
Professor of Mental Health
The Queen's University of Belfast

Preface

The idea to write this book arose after we had just completed the MRCPsych examination. Our close proximity to the examination has, we hope, helped us to focus in on the needs of those studying for the examination. We felt that the texts available for Patient Management Problems failed to represent the style of questions and answers expected. In particular the purpose of the book was to help those working in areas where an opportunity to work with other candidates was limited and to give them a guide to the manner in which answers should be delivered.

We would like to thank all those who have encouraged us in the field of psychiatry, both as an interest and career.

Specifically we would like to thank Dr G. McDonald and Dr J. Coates for their constructive criticism of the text, Mrs B. McCoy for patience in providing all the secretarial work and to all the others with whom we work, who made the task easier. Not least of all, we thank Professor Roy McClelland who has kindly provided our book with a foreword.

Paul H. McCrea
Joanne D.E. Weir

December, 1993

Introduction

The Patient Management oral has been a feature of the M.R.C.Psych. Part II examination since the inception of the new format in 1988. The College places great emphasis on this component of the examination and candidates need to be well prepared. The object is not merely to test a candidate's knowledge but also his judgement, skill and ability to act in a common sense manner. The examiners are able to assess how a candidate would handle ethical and medico-legal problems and many, although knowledgable, fail this part of the examination. To try to redress the balance, several books have been published. In our opinion, it is difficult, in a book, to reproduce accurately the format of the examination and it is easy to become over-inclusive and excessively detailed in the answers.

Most candidates are given four problems in their 30 minute oral – 2 from each examiner. Examiners are encouraged to produce real cases from their own portfolios. Most ask an initial question and then provide more information as the oral progresses, so allowing the candidate to work through the problem just as he would were he faced with it in his clinical practice. We have tried to reproduce this sequence in our book. All our problems are based on real cases we have experienced. We have divided the book into 12 papers of 4 questions each. Although the majority relates to adult mental illness, all the sub-specialities are represented. Most questions are followed up by "supplementaries" to direct the candidate along a certain line of thought. We have not attempted to provide exhaustive or detailed answers: rather we are attempting to teach a framework that the candidate can use in his answers. We believe that one should answer the problem as if it were a real situation – therefore it is important to gather all the information, to act methodically and systematically and avoid jumping to conclusions. The candidate must endeavour to demonstrate that he would be safe and reliable in his clinical practice. It is not essential to reach the "right" diagnosis – indeed there might not be a "right" diagnosis, but what is important is to demonstrate an ability to think clearly and sensibly when faced with a clinical conundrum. Direct questions should not be evaded nor should the candidate waffle – however an examiner who presents what he considers a difficult problem of his own may be taken aback if the candidate begins his answer with "well, this is obviously a case of ....".

We have assumed a good background knowledge and relevant experience in our readers. We feel this book will be of most use to those candidates who are within six months of sitting the Part II examination. We do not believe it is a substitute either for clinical experience or for practice orals with a senior colleague or Clinical Tutor. Most candidates will find it helpful to work in pairs – one asking the question and the other answering.

We have tried to produce answers that are compatible with current teaching. Some readers may disagree with what we have written. Remember, however, that in psychiatry seldom is anything clearly right or wrong. It is not necessary that the examiner agree wholeheartedly with everything you say provided what you say is sensible and that you can support it. The problems are not meant to be easy and we have avoided excessive detail and length in our answers. If we have made serious errors we can only apologise and crave our readers' indulgence.

When asked a question – listen carefully, ask the examiner to repeat it if necessary, think clearly and work through the information methodically. Do not worry if the question is broad or vague: the examiner will fill in the gaps as the oral progresses. Above all, keep calm and appear sensible. Looking the part is very important. And remember, common things are common.

We apologize to anyone who is offended by our use of "he" or "his" throughout when either gender's personal pronoun or possessive adjective could be used. Nothing should be read into this and candidates can answer using whichever gender they please.

Good luck!

Q1

A Registrar from the ENT team requests that you see one of their patients – a 36 year old separated Chinese chef who has recently lost his job due to gambling. He received radiotherapy six months previously for nasopharyngeal carcinoma and is now complaining of difficulty in swallowing. The nursing staff has noted that he is withdrawn and uncommunicative and is worried that he might be depressed.

a) How would you manage the situation?

b) The Consultant is of the opinion that the malignancy has recurred and that no curative treatment can be offered.

c) The patient expresses concern about his terminal care and implies that he might wish to end his life.

A1

a) Determine whether the patient understands English. Obtain a translator if necessary.

You need to know as much as possible from the ward staff about his physical state:

ability to eat/speak;	nutritional status;
sleep pattern;	extent and spread of his disease.

Then see patient: take a full history and carry out a mental state examination. Look especially for:

evidence of depression;   possible organic brain syndrome; possible underlying psychosis.

Find out what medication (if any) he has been given.

What is he worried about?

You need to determine:

what he has been told about his illness and what he fears and believes (note cultural and religious factors); is there an underlying mental illness?

b) You need to know if the patient has been told this.

What are the plans for palliative treatment? The patient needs to be informed as to the extent of his illness and the options.

He needs psychological support to accept the diagnosis and adjust accordingly. Ward Staff – Medical and Nursing – might require support in their attempts to adjust.

His family may also request help.

c) It is important to clarify and alleviate his fears.

Good communication must be fostered between patient and staff.

Involvement of specialists in terminal care would be beneficial.

The patient needs reassurance that pain control will be adequate and will not be required to be "earned".

Any underlying depressive illness would require appropriate treatment.

Use of an antidepressant may alleviate chronic pain.

The patient's dignity and self respect are paramount.

Q2

You are asked to see at her home a 32 year old married mother of a 2 year old child. The mother is almost housebound by her fear of dirt and is constantly cleaning.

You learn she had an episode of depression shortly after the birth of the child.

a) What diagnoses would you be considering?

b) What questions would you be interested in asking her?

c) How would you treat her?

A2

a) The likely diagnoses are:
    depression;
    obsessive-compulsive disorder;
    another mental illness;

You still need a full history and examination

Obtain a collateral account to aid diagnosis

A period of observation of her behavioural pattern would be beneficial.

b) Particular areas of interest would be:
    why does she do it? (to distinguish between obsessional and delusional behaviour);
    why has she become so incapacitated? (try to find a cause);
    what was her previous level of function?
    what her mood is, particularly any suggestion of guilt, unworthiness or suicidal ideation;
    what her attitude to her child is. If this is poor, other agencies may need to be involved.

c) Treatment of what is likely to be an underlying primary depressive illness is as follows:
    explanation, advice, reassurance;
    arrange increased support;
    antidepressants, e.g. selective serotonin re-uptake inhibitors or clomipramine.

    (consider admission and/or ECT if severe)

    When her mood has improved, behavioural therapy may be required.

Q3

You are called by a practice manager to do a domiciliary visit on an 82 year old woman. She has been found wandering by her neighbours.

a) How will you respond?

b) You agree to go to see her, what will you do?

A3

a) The suggestion is of a confusional state either acute or chronic.

Try to find out as much background information as possible:
  why has the practice manager requested a visit? You would need a request from the General Practitioner (GP);
  what does the lady's GP think? Has he seen her?

b) 1. Try to arrange a visit so that an informant will also be available.

Attempt to take a history.

Perform a mental state examination with special emphasis on cognitive assessment.

Examine her physically to rule out a physical illness.
Examine medication – what drugs, how often: does the patient know what they are and when to take them?

Look at living conditions and the lady's personal appearance.

Assess what supports are like – is there a carer?

Assess the risks to herself and others.

If acute confusional state is the likely diagnosis: why is this?

Liaise with GP

Consider medical domiciliary visit or admission

You might follow up later on as there may be an underlying chronic organic brain state

2. If it is a chronic brain syndrome:
  why has she deteriorated?
  would she require admission?
  does she need medication?
  can she remain at home?

In these circumstances you might liaise with her local care manager and be part of a multidisciplinary assessment about future support and care.

Q4

A plastic surgeon refers to you a 27 year old woman who complains her nose is too large; she is requesting surgery.

a) How would you proceed?

b) You feel her nose is normal. She becomes aggressive and accuses you of staring at her and laughing at her. She states that everyone knows about her nose and pokes fun at her.

c) The woman returns some time later in a rage. She says the surgeon has refused to treat her and blames you. She insists on reading the notes you wrote about her.

A4

a) Obtain as much evidence of her odd beliefs from the surgeon as possible:

> why does he wish her to see a psychiatrist and is she agreeable to do so?

Arrange to see her for full history and examination and also obtain an informant's history – look for evidence of mental illness or substance abuse.

Is there:
> low self esteem?
> depression?
> schizophrenia?

In dysmorphophobia the person believes that part of his body is abnormal, but often has poor insight and refuses treatment.

b) Clearly the patient is extremely distressed. A sympathetic approach and tactful handling of the situation is necessary. Clarify the details of the beliefs.

Look for evidence of:
> delusions, especially of reference;
> hallucinations.

Her comments suggest delusions of reference and possible auditory hallucinations. Look for suicidal ideas or depressive content.

c) Try to persuade her of the sincerity of your involvement.

Do your best to calm the situation. A patient is now entitled to see the notes providing you believe his health will not be damaged by so doing. Therefore it is important to make careful notes. You should not hand them to her for perusal but give her the contact number of the appropriate administrator who handles such requests. Most hospitals and units now have a leaflet outlining how a patient is able to look at his or her own notes.

Tell the GP and surgeon the situation. The patient may be persuaded to take medication or to consult another psychiatrist. However the patient often refuses treatment.

PAPER II

Q1
Late one night a neighbour consults you in great distress. He has discovered that his 13 year old daughter has just attempted to take her own life.

a) How would you deal with this?

b) Two days later, the girl's form mistress telephones you and says she believes the girl has been sexually abused. She asks your advice on how to proceed.

A1

a) Ask the neighbour to tell you clearly what has happened to assess whether emergency medical attention is needed.

   Go to the girl:
   attend to any injury that requires emergency aid, e.g. clear airway, maintain respiration, arrest any haemorrhage.

   If necessary ring for ambulance or contact GP.

   If it is a relatively minor injury the family should be calmed down and their GP contacted for appointment or visit. Ensure that they are aware you are not taking on the child's care in spite of great concern.

b) Clarify with the teacher that you are not the doctor responsible for the girl's care, and that her correct course of action is to contact the GP who will advise her appropriately.

Q2

A 60 year old man is referred to you by his solicitor. He is facing charges of indecent exposure towards young girls in a nearby park.

a) What would you need to know?

b) The man is quite shocked and distressed by it all. He claims he has never done this before and states that it is quite out of character.

c) He is terrified his family will find out and says he will commit suicide if he goes to court.

   What would you do?

A2

a) To begin with you need to clarify the nature of the solicitor's referral and details of the charge.

Arrange to see the man for full history and examination. Request full access to medical and psychiatric notes and ask for an informant's history.

Note:
premorbid personality, e.g. passive, obsessional, enjoys risk-taking;
mental illness – depression and brain damage or other stressful life events;
psychosexual history:
sexual dysfunction,   orientation,
quality of relationships,   usual sexual practice.

You need to know details of incident(s), onset, frequency, and whether:
impulsive or planned;
flaccid or erect penis or associated masturbation;
guilt or pleasure after incident;
age of those exposed to;
attempts to contact victim.

b) A history from an informant is needed to confirm premorbid personality and behaviour, and confirm any change in these or mood. This will help decide the cause of his behaviour and might help to suggest treatment.

c) You need to assess his mental state:
is he depressed?   is he a suicidal risk?
is there another mental illness?
These could be causal or a result of his behaviour.

If depressed, he will need appropriate treatment – anti-depressant and/or ECT plus supportive psychotherapy.

If he has another mental illness this will require treatment.

He may require a place of safety depending on the extent of public knowledge.

If he is not depressed and not mentally ill, he may be trying to avoid a court appearance. You would furnish your report and advise the solicitor accordingly.

You would not be in a position to offer treatment unless the GP refers him back to you.

Q3

You are asked to see a 48 year old man who suffers from bouts of severe depression of mood lasting a few days at a time. During these spells he is distressed by suicidal and homicidal thoughts.

a) What would you do?

b) There is no evidence of alcohol abuse. He is currently well and is troubled only every few months. He states that he will never consider admission, no matter how ill he becomes.

What management would you use?

A3

a) Begin by taking a full history and examination. Try to obtain as much collateral information as possible.

Try to speak to his GP.

Particular areas of interest would be:
    1. length of time affected and previous acts of violence;
    2. precipitants;
    3. any manic phases;
    4. treatment offered;
    5. drug/alcohol history;
    6. relevant family history.

Possibilities are:
    1. affective disorder, (rapid cycling);
    2. alcohol/drug abuse;
    3. personality disorder;
    4. depression secondary to physical illness, e.g. epilepsy;
    5. other mental illness.

After appropriate investigation and arrival at diagnosis, the plan would be to assess his current mental state and decide on treatment in both short term and long term.

b) 1. Regular follow up by community psychiatric nurse. Ensure relatives are well informed about what to look out for.

2. Look at antecedents and precipitants to try and predict.

3. May need increased support at times of illness.

4. Even if not willing, admission may still be required under mental health legislation when ill.

5. Advise on removal of dangerous items in his environment.

6. If he has an affective disorder:
    drugs – consider antidepressants, both curative and prophylactically; beware of overdose potential;
    consider lithium or carbamazepine (if rapid cycling).

Q4

You are asked to see a 21 year old woman who has dropped out of law school. She is referred to you from a local hospital. She was admitted there after being found incontinent and unconscious.

They tell you that she has been attending her GP who suspected anorexia due to her poor food intake (and a low blood sugar was noted on admission).

How would you manage her?

A4

Despite the way the question is phrased, the first step in management would be to obtain as much information as possible:

full history, examination;
speak to relative;
speak to ward staff and GP;
consider report from university tutor.

The history is suggestive of an epileptic type seizure.
You need to ask why; you need to rule out drugs overdose due to suicidal intent:

what have the medical staff diagnosed?
is there any personal or family history of epilepsy?
does she take drugs and/or abuse alcohol?
why was she attending GP and why did he suspect anorexia nervosa? (Note: low blood sugar would not support anorexia nervosa)

You would also need to know why she dropped out of law school:

Is there a family history of mental illness?

What are the social supports like?

Management is in two parts:

1. Management and investigation of seizure (if this was what it was):

is it epilepsy of idiopathic nature?
is it due to alcohol/drugs?
is there an underlying medical problem?

The role of the psychiatrist in the last instance would be to provide support if required.

2. Management of any underlying mental illness or behaviour/addiction as appropriate, e.g. depression, anorexia nervosa, drug or alcohol abuse or addiction.

PAPER III

Q1

A 72 year old woman is referred to you by her GP with symptoms of weepiness, low mood and lack of interest.

a) How would you investigate her?

b) Her husband died suddenly, while she was out, over a year ago. They had been happily married for nearly fifty years.

c) She still lays the table and prepares meals for him. The bedroom they shared remains untouched since he died. She has never visited the grave and finds it difficult to accept that he is gone.

A1

a) First clarify with the GP the reason for referral, has the woman been unresponsive to treatment or was he unclear of the diagnosis?

Arrange to see the woman for full history and examination and ask for an informant's history as well as obtaining access to medical and psychiatric records.

Look for evidence of:
    mental illness, especially depression;
    dementia;
    physical illness.

Remember the woman may be suffering from a grief reaction.

b) You need details of the quality of the relationship, nature of husband's illness, suddenness of death, feelings of guilt, nature of grief, whether she attended the funeral, etc. Determine whether she was previously unwell and whether he was the carer.

c) The history is suggestive of pathological grief but she may also be clinically depressed.

Does she require in-patient or out-patient treatment?

She may require:
    antidepressants or ECT;
    supportive psychotherapy possibly by CPN;
    bereavement counselling (CPN);
    rule out organic disorder, assess physical wellbeing;
    assess capacity of self care – involve relatives and Social Services;
    day care or social outlets.

Q2

A GP refers a middle-aged couple to you. They are concerned about their 14 year old daughter who has become unruly, is staying out late and is drinking and taking drugs.

a) What would you do?

b) The girl herself comes to see you. She is quiet in the interview but states she is fed up with her parents' rows and intends to leave home as soon as possible.

c) The parents admit that their marriage is experiencing difficulties.

How would you proceed?

A2

a) Find out as much as possible about the family:
>   the quality of parental relationships;
>   the health of other children (and their behaviour);
>   any history of alcohol or drug abuse in the family?
>   any criminal record in the family?

See the parents. You will need a full history. Ask them to bring their daughter along too.

You would need to see her too and clarify:
>   her view of her behaviour: how much? how often?
>   any changes – at home, at school;
>   schooling record;
>   when problems began exactly;
>   her view of her family.

Look for alcohol use and into her parents' marital relationship.

Is there evidence of mental illness in the girl (or her parents)?

Observe the parental interaction with their daughter.

b) Behavioural changes in children often reflect parental or family discord. Discuss with her options to change herself and options for her family, e.g. marital counselling.

c) Involve all the family.

Identify the marital difficulties:
>   consider the parents for marital therapy – either yourself or elsewhere, e.g. Relate);
>   address addictive behaviour or mental illness in the parents;
>   advise on support of relatives, e.g. Al-Anon;
>   treat the girl's addictive behaviour, provide psychological support and treat any mental illness;
>   encourage her to remain at home unless this is divisive.

Q3

You are asked to see a 21 year old girl with a history of bingeing, vomiting, starving and cutting her arms.

a) How would you manage her?

b) You subsequently find out that she is adopted and met her biological mother 18 months ago. Her biological mother suffers from chronic schizophrenia.

   How does this affect your management?

A3

a) Start with a full history and examination, obtain collateral information. The history points to an eating disorder and at least one episode of deliberate self harm.

   You should concentrate on:
   1. Obtaining as much information about the eating disorder with the aim of trying to categorise her and find out how long the problem has been with her.
   2. Obtain information about her deliberate self harm. When? How often? What means? Why? How she feels before and after? Was it a serious suicide attempt?
   3. Is there evidence of a clear underlying depressive illness or another mental illness?

   The management is then:
   1. Examination, advice, reassurance; develop trust BUT NOT OVER-RELIANCE.
   Try to treat her eating disorder along cognitive behavioural lines. This needs accurate diagnosis and identification of underlying psychological conflicts.
   Separation issues are invariably paramount.
   2. Treat any underlying depressive illness appropriately.
   3. Repeated deliberate self harm should be managed behaviourally and the individual should be encouraged to seek other means of relief of tension/boredom.

b) This may be irrelevant, extremely relevant or moderately so. It depends on when and how she found out she was adopted and how she felt. The relationship with her adoptive family is important.

   Who decided to meet whom; what did the patient know about her mother before the meeting? You also need to know how often they have met and what the relationship is like?

   Here explain the diagnosis to the patient.

   When the eating disorder is controlled, explore any concerns she may have about her mother's or her own future.

   Look at issues of guilt, shame or low self esteem.

   Compare the issues of fantasy mother with real mother. This issue is likely to complicate treatment and would probably require psychological follow-up for a number of years.

Q4

You are asked to see a 19 year old unemployed man. A month earlier he was sitting on a bus when a man pulled out a gun and shot the person he was sitting beside.

The patient now complains of fear and anxiety and believes his own life is in danger.

a) What diagnoses would you be considering?

b) How would you diagnose post traumatic stress disorder (PTSD) and how would you manage it?

A4

a) Diagnoses to be considered would be:
>   a stress reaction;
>   an anxiety neurosis;
>   a depressive illness;
>   another mental illness.

Substance abuse, particularly alcohol, might be another factor.

The diagnosis would be much clearer after a full history, examination and collateral history.

Important points are:
>   did his problems predate the incident or not?
>   is his belief that his own life is in danger delusional or not? (he may have a real basis for his fear);
>   what is his normal premorbid personality?
>   did he know the victim and/or the gunman?
>   is he a danger to himself or others?

b) To diagnose PTSD you require (DSM IIIR):
>   1. a severe psychological trauma usually outside normal experience;
>   2. evidence of intrusive recollections, re-living the experience etc.;
>   3. avoidance of similar situations or talking about it;
>   4. evidence of hyperarousal and suggestions of a change in personality and low level of functioning;
>   5. symptoms persisting for at least one month.

The management is mainly psychological and social. (Any underlying depressive illness should be treated appropriately):
>   allow the person to ventilate;
>   provide psychological support;
>   use simple behavioural techniques to reverse the avoidance components of the illness, allied to use of relaxation methods;
>   the patient will benefit from reassurance that he is not unusual, odd or malingering;
>   relatives need advice and reassurance – to be supportive yet encouraging;
>   drug treatments, at present, have little to offer.

Q1

Your are asked to see a 31 year old anorexic girl. Her weight has fallen below an agreed weight of 32 kilograms after which she is admitted to hospital.

a) How would you manage her care (she has a 20 year duration of illness)?

b) She refuses admission.

How would you proceed?

A1

a) This girl is chronically affected by anorexia nervosa and will be under a contract. You need to know what the other components are.

Establish a relationship (if you do not already know her).

Take a full history and examination.

Weigh her.

Find out:
   1. why her weight has dropped, i.e. cause?
   2. how it has fallen, i.e. method?
   3. is there any underlying depression or suicidal ideation?

Because of the duration, a "cure" is not a reasonable option. She should be admitted to hospital as part of her behavioural contract. Other components are likely to be:
   supervised caring/bed-rest until weight is put on again;
   use of positive reinforcement may be helpful;
   often the patient co-operates fully and puts on weight;
   depression should be treated;
   underlying psychological conflicts should be addressed;
   mutual trust must be maintained;
   beware of physical sequelae and look for same;

b) In this event you must ask why she refuses admission? She may lack confidence in you or herself; she may feel "fed up" and that the whole effort is pointless.

With time and empathy you may be able to reverse her decision.

If this is unsuccessful you may have to arrange for her formal admission under the Mental Health Legislation.

Even in the absence of definite depression or suicidal intent this is still justified.

Furthermore, you would also be justified in passing a nasogastric tube and forcing nutrition on her. The rationale here is that the patient is at substantial risk and her ability to make a decision is impaired due to a mental disorder.

Q2

A 55 year old man is admitted following an episode when he brutally attacked his niece with a hammer in the early hours of the morning whilst she lay in her bed.
Examination reveals spider naevi and gynaecomastia.

How would you assess this man's dangerousness?

A2

a) You require a full history and examination. You would also like to speak to his niece and another informant and to his GP.

Particular areas of interest would be:
   any family history of mental illness, alcohol abuse or violence?
   any personal history of the same three factors?
   how many attacks have occurred, over what period?
   who has been attacked?
   were there any obvious precipitants?
   were alcohol or drugs involved?
   the exact circumstances of the attack and the injuries sustained.

You also need to determine what the man remembers (if anything) about the attack:
   why did he do it?
   has he attacked other people?
   how did he feel afterwards and how he feels now?

Likely possibilities are:
   1. alcohol or drug intoxication or withdrawal;
   2. mental illness – delusions, hallucinations telling him to do it;
   3. organic illness, e.g. epilepsy, brain damage, dementing illness;
   4. other, e.g. episodic dyscontrol or severe personality disorder.

The history suggests alcohol abuse is a factor. It may be causative or it could be co-incidential.

Your aim would be to establish a cause.

His dangerousness would depend on:
   1. the cause and whether treatment would be helpful;
   2. the number, frequency and severity of assaults;
   3. any mental illness;
   4. the likelihood of abstinence from alcohol;
   5. the person's insight and degree of self control.

A period of in-patient observation might be beneficial allied to education concerning alcohol and help to abstain.

In the absence of a mental illness which would impair his judgement, the man should be handled by the judicial process.

Q3

You are asked to assess a 15 year old boy who is facing charges of joyriding.

a) What would you do?

b) The request comes from the boy's GP, who tells you the boy comes from a broken home and has been raised by an aunt who is alcoholic.

c) The boy admits to other criminal offences and says he cannot help himself.

A3

a) Clarify the source of referral, i.e. GP or legal? Why was assessment sought.

Take a full history and examination. Speak to an informant and obtain as much collateral information as possible.

Particularly important are:
   any family history of alcohol or drug abuse?
   is there marital or family disharmony?
   what is his school record?
   where did his behaviour begin and has he any other relevant features in his forensic history?
   is there evidence of mental illness in himself or his family?

b) You will need further information

The parents:
   why they separated and when?
   is there a history of parental violence or criminal activity?
   what is the present contact with his parents and other family members?

The aunt:
   assess her level of alcohol dependence;
   what is the quality of her relationship with the young man?
   is there evidence that she is mentally ill?

c) This suggests he is beginning to develop a degree of trust.
   What is his attitude to:
   car theft?
   his other activities?
   his aunt?
   his parents?
   his future?

He appears to lack stable adult influences and examples.
Consider:
   increased level of access to his parents and other family members;
   assess whether he needs assistance at school;
   treat any physical or mental illness;
   referral to a sympathetic Social Worker or voluntary agency.

He might benefit from involvement with a therapeutic community approach.

Consider referring aunt for help with her alcohol abuse.

Q4

You are asked to see a 72 year old man in a medical ward who was admitted with an exacerbation of his chronic airways obstruction. The physician complains that the patient is disruptive and unco-operative, and that the patient believes that the staff are trying to kill him; he is refusing to eat in case his food is poisoned.

a) How would you proceed with this case?

b) The patient has no relevant past psychiatric history. He was not paranoid on admission and has been in hospital for over two weeks. Recently his treatment was changed.

c) In addition to nebulised and oral bronchodilators, a short course of steroids was commenced along with a broad spectrum antibiotic given intravenously.

A4

a) This is suggestive of an acute confusional state.

An examination and mental state assessment are required. Find out as much as possible from Ward Staff and his notes. Speak to an informant who knew him prior to admission.

You need to know the nature of his physical illness and what medications he has been, and is, receiving.

Possible causes include:
1. infection, e.g. pneumonia or UTI;
2. hypoxia or increased PCO_2, e.g. due to COAD;
3. heart failure or a myocardial infarct;
4. a CVA;
5. diabetes mellitus.

Find out if there is a history of alcohol abuse; make sure his condition is not due to alcohol (or drug) withdrawal.

You need to identify and treat the cause – if possible.

N.B. neuroleptics can be used to settle agitation and paranoia.

Nurse in well lit room, familiar staff, frequent reassurance, etc.

b) This makes alcohol withdrawal or an underlying psychiatric illness very unlikely.

Why was his treatment changed? What changes occurred? Are these relevant?

c) Steroids can precipitate a psychotic illness as can some antibiotics.

The use of i.v. antibiotics suggests a severe infection and it may be this which is the cause – any illness should be treated vigorously.

Steroids should be withdrawn as quickly as possible.

Neuroleptics should be continued cautiously until mental state returns to normal.

Follow-up psychiatric care is likely to be required.

PAPER V

Q1

A police surgeon telephones you one night when you are on call. He has been summoned to the local airport and has just seen a 24 year old man who has barricaded himself in the arrivals lounge, claiming that the "second coming" is about to happen.

a) How would you deal with this case?

b) A relative has been contacted who informs you that the young man has been behaving oddly for some time, gave up his well paid job and has complained that God has been speaking to him.

c) The young man is initially co-operative but then becomes aggressive and refuses to leave. The airport is becoming crowded and passengers are beginning to lose their tempers.

What would you do?

A1

a) Obtain as much information as possible:
   is the individual local?
   in this case, try to contact his GP and/or family;
   did he have a relative or friend accompanying him?
   is there a history of:
      drug abuse or alcohol; mental illness; organic illness
      (e.g. TLE)?

If the individual is foreign, you may need a translator and a consular official present. The Airport Police should be able to help.

Next you need to decide immediately about dangerousness:
   has there been violence or is there a risk?
   are hostages involved?
   does he have a weapon.

There is a suggestion of a delusional belief. Possibilities include a schizophrenic-like illness or a drug induced psychosis.

b) This suggests a decline in function and the presence of hallucinations. This supports a psychiatric illness. He is likely to be unpredictable and would benefit from a period of hospital assessment.

c) Ensure Police are present but not too obvious. Have the area cordoned off. Obtain the help of experienced staff, especially with a psychiatric background.

Remain calm; try and avoid any sudden or precipitous activity.

The presence of the GP or relative may reassure the patient.

You should try to persuade the patient to give himself up and be admitted to a mental hospital.

Take time and do not rush the patient.

Emergency neuroleptic medication and sufficient force in keeping with the law may be necessary.

If required, the Mental Health Legislation can be invoked.

Q2

A 66 year old man is admitted to a medical ward as an emergency. He has a long history of alcohol abuse but recently has reduced his consumption. He has become agitated, restless and suspicious.

a) How would you deal with him?

b) After a few days his physical condition improves but he remains paranoid and appears to be hallucinating.

c) Eventually he settles on medication and requests discharge.

   How would you follow him up and what advice would you give?

A2

a) The history would lead you to consider the possibility of the onset of withdrawal progressing to delirium tremens. A full history and examination is necessary. Previous psychiatric and medical notes should be obtained and an informant's history obtained as soon as possible.

N.B. A diagnosis of withdrawal requires treatment with benzodiazepines, usually chlordiazepoxide; management of dehydration, which is often present; appropriate diet and vitamins (and an anticonvulsant if there is a history of seizures).

Rule out other causes of acute confusional states which can occur coincidentally:
   infection – pneumonia, UTI;
   hypoxia;
   head injury – subdural.

Assess for mental illness, e.g. dementia, schizophrenia.

b) Reassess his physical condition and mental state.

Admit him to a psychiatric unit for assessment and observation to clarify his symptoms.

Consider:
   schizophrenia, paraphrenia;
   organic dementia;
   medication – change of, or commencement of, treatment for alcoholic hallucinosis.

Neuroleptics should be considered if his symptoms persist or are distressing.

c) The diagnosis is probably Alcohol Induced Psychosis. He probably can be taken off his medication but he should be carefully followed up and should be warned of the risks of a further psychotic episode if he consumes alcohol. Advise abstinence from alcohol with support from education and AA groups.

The community psychiatric nurse should be involved.

Inform GP and family concerning diagnosis and follow up.

Social Services may also need to be involved if there are problems with accommodation or self care.

Q3
A 45 year old man is referred to you again for anxiety symptoms. He previously attended the Day Hospital for relaxation therapy and anxiety management.

a) How would you manage him?

b) His problem surfaced again with changing demands in his job.

   What would you advise?

A3

a) Begin with a full history, examination and perusal of his past notes:

> find out what symptoms he has;
> compare these with his previous symptoms;
> ask how he managed while at the Day Hospital;
> it is likely he either:
>> recovered;
>
> or
>> improved after attendance at Day Hospital, but has now relapsed – in this case ask why? Has he used relaxation?
>
> or
>> failed to improve after attendance at the Anxiety Management Group and despite use of relaxation.

In both cases you need to:

> 1. confirm the diagnosis;
>   rule out any physical disease e.g. thyroid disease;
>   rule out any other mental illness e.g. depression;
>   rule out substance abuse.
>
> 2. Identify any precipitants or perpetuating factors.

The management is then:

> treat any underlying mental illness/substance abuse;
> refer to GP /physician if physical cause suspected;
> reconsider anxiety management and relaxation and/or anxiolytic therapy – beware of dependence;
> consider psychological/social support to deal with causative factors.

b) Here you need to know what his employment is and what changes have occurred.

Either his reaction to the changes is understandable or not! The latter this suggests he is not functioning to his normal level. Why?

Consider options:

> 1. return to normal employment;
> 2. less demanding role;
> 3. change employment.

He may require a period off work during the initial component of his treatment.

Q4

You are asked to see a 59 year old married man by his GP. For some time he has feared that, when out for a walk, he will cause damage to other peoples' property making it necessary to go back to apologise.

What are the possible diagnoses and how would you manage him (no actual damage is caused)?

A4

First take a full history and make a complete examination.

Speak to his wife and his GP.

You know no actual damage is caused – is the patient aware of this or not? Are these fears obsessional in nature or not? Is he generally anxious?

Possible diagnoses are:
1. obsessive compulsive disorder;
2. depressive illness in an obsessional personality with increase in obsessionality;
3. organic brain disease, e.g. dementia;
4. psychotic illness – with delusional beliefs;
5. anxiety disorder.

How long has the disorder been manifest? Try to elicit details of his premorbid personality. What are his actual fears; do they extend to people as well as property?

What effect is it having on his daily life?

The management depends on the underlying cause.

Depression or psychosis need treatment. Discuss the nature of the illness with his wife.
(Consider admission).

An O.C.D. requires behavioural treatment.

Here there seem to be rituals as well as ruminations. Rituals respond best to response prevention – exposure to environmental cues with resistance on the part of the patient. Ruminations usually improve as the rituals become less prominent.

Modelling, prompting and setting of time limits are required. A co-therapist is necessary. His wife might be suitable. (Consider using a community psychiatric nurse to support both husband and wife).

Ruminations on their own may be more problematic. Thought stopping and thought satiation have both been suggested with varying degrees of success.

Clomipramine and S.S.R.I. may be helpful in some cases, especially those with marked depressive features.

PAPER VI

Q1

You are asked by a GP to see a 41 year old woman with a fear of birds. It has been present for years but has become a greater problem recently.

a) What approach would you take?

b) Her husband started a new business three years ago and she left her job to work with him. This is the only change in the history.

What treatment would you offer?

A1

a) As with any new case the first requirements are:
    full history and examination;
    speak to informant;
    consult all previous notes.

The history is of a specific phobia. The patient has apparently coped until recently. Why is this?

You need to identify:
    1. any obvious changes which might have increased general stress or anxiety, e.g. move of house, change in aspects of marital relationship or
    2. changes related to the phobia e.g. move to countryside, neighbour keeping pigeons etc.

You would also need to rule out a depressive illness or the development of an anxiety neurosis.

b) This informs us of a major life event three years ago.

You need to see if the change in her phobia bears a temporal relationship to this:
    how is the business doing?
    where does she work? what does she do exactly?
    is she coping?
    what effect has it had on her marital relationship?

The treatment would be:
    1. Establish a psychotherapeutic relationship with the aim of:
       a) identifying stressors;
       b) advising appropriate adjustments to relieve stressors; this may involve use of relaxation or other techniques;
    2. recruit support of husband;
    3. treat any underlying depressive illness;
    4. specific behaviour therapy related to the phobia may be helpful but it is likely that other adjustments and treatment will produce improvement before behaviour therapy is required. Exposure *in vivo* is the treatment of choice in specific phobias.

Q2
You are asked to see a 78 year old man by his GP. He has been aggressive to his wife and follows her around.

a) How do you proceed?

b) He is a diabetic but is refusing to keep to his diet and is now incontinent of urine.

c) His wife feels she cannot cope any longer.

What would you advise?

A2

a) Take a full history and examination.

(It may be beneficial to see the patient in his own home.) Get his wife's account and try to speak to another informant in case it is inaccurate. Get as much information as possible from his GP.

Try to observe husband and wife together.

Find out how long this behaviour has been going on and whether the aggression is physical/verbal or both. Has anything provoked it? Is it related to an apparent seizure?

Look out for delusions, hallucinations or suggestions of morbid jealousy:
    has he a past history of psychiatric illness?
    does he abuse alcohol?
    is he violent or aggressive to anyone else?
    what is his premorbid personality?
    is he on medication or has his medication been changed?
    is the husband aware beforehand that he will be violent?
    is he aware during violence?
    has he any memory afterwards; is he remorseful?

The possibilities are:
    1. mental illness – depression, dementia, alcohol abuse, paranoid state, other;
    2. physical illness – stroke, brain tumour, metabolic disorder;
    3. no mental or physical illness – here there is little you can do beyond general advice and behavioural management.

b) Discover more about his diabetes from his GP or diabetologist; it may have worsened and caused some or all of his problems; or an underlying mental or physical illness may be causing non-compliance.

Admission for assessment would be helpful: either under a psychiatrist or his diabetologist if his diabetic state is severely deranged.

c) This is an understandable initial reaction.

Advise that she wait and see what cause is found and how he responds to treatment.

A phased discharge with increased support could be tried. However, his physical or mental condition may preclude this, he may be non-compliant; if so, the wife should meet a sympathetic social worker to discuss future options.

Q3
A distraught mother is referred to you. Her 7 year old daughter
has begun to wet the bed at night.

a) What would you do?

b) The GP tells you all physical investigations are negative.
    The family deny any emotional problem.

c) A behavioural approach does not work. The mother tells
    you that the child has become more withdrawn.

d) The girl herself eventually tells you a neighbour's boy has
    been "touching her down below".

    How would you proceed?

A3

a) It is unusual for a child with enuresis to be referred to a psychiatrist. Therefore you must obtain details of what the referring agent requires and obtain as much information as possible on both the child and mother:

    1. have the child examined by the GP or paediatrician if necessary to rule out physical illness;

    2. obtain a full history from the mother, observe them together and obtain informant's history from the father.

It is important to determine onset and any recent changes at home or at school and whether there have been any changes in behaviour as well.

b) Arrange to see the parents together and separately. If the parents deny problems talk to the GP to determine if he has any knowledge of family discord, alcohol problems etc.

Ask the parents if you can have a report from the child's teacher to determine if problems are arising in school.

Offer a star chart and follow with a bell and pad if required. Careful explanation of problem to parents improves the success of treatment.

c) Arrange to see the child again with the mother. The issue of abuse should be considered, though at this stage you have no apparent evidence. Provide an environment which will help the child to communicate, e.g. drawings.

Is her withdrawn state due to a mental illness or another cause?

d) Clarify with the child what she is saying without leading questions.

Determine the age of the boy.

Refer the child to the Child Protection Unit of the Social Services, informing the parents of your intentions.

Contact the GP and ensure adquate psychological support is provided for the girl and her family.

Q4

A 57 year old publican consults you at the suggestion of his GP. He admits to abusing alcohol and requests your help in establishing "controlled drinking".

a) What advice would you give?

b) Some days later the GP telephones you. He states he gave the patient a referral letter (which you never received). The GP's main concern is the publican's morbid jealousy towards his wife who is 25 years his junior.

c) The patient denies he is morbidly jealous and claims he is the laughing stock of his customers. He states that his wife is having numerous affairs and he intends to find the truth, no matter what it takes to get her to confess.

Q1
You are asked to see a 30 year old teacher, diabetic since 9 years of age with very poor control. She has admitted to manipulating her insulin to keep her weight down.

How would you deal with this referral?

A1

The referral would be dealt with in the usual fashion:
full history and examination;
obtain collateral information;
look at medical notes;
speak to her physician.

You would be particularly interested in features of:
1. weight control – what other methods she uses and how she views these;
2. an eating disorder;
3. a depressive illness;
4. another mental illness.

You would need to assess the level of social support and the degree of stress that the teacher is under in her personal and professional life.

N.B. It is well to remember that patients with any serious chronic illness are often capable of manipulation of their illness.

You need to decide:
a. if there is any underlying mental illness;
b. if there is no underlying mental illness, why is this lady behaving like this?

Treatment needs to be carried out in conjunction with the physician who looks after her diabetes.
1. Check that she understands the nature of her diabetes and its management and the need for good control.
2. Identify any stressors and try to deal with them appropriately.
3. Treat any underlying mental illness or coincidenal physical illness.
4. Ensure she is receiving adequate support. Advise on support groups.

Q2

A 32 year old woman who has a 7 year history of manic depressive psychosis attends your clinic. She wishes to stop lithium treatment which she has been on for the last 5 years.

a) What approach would you take?

b) Three weeks later her GP contacts you saying the woman is depressed and suicidal.

   What do you do?

A2

a) The suggestion is that the woman is well known to you. Nonetheless you would still need to have a full background history, as much collateral information as possible and an up-to-date mental state assessment to hand.

   You would particularly want to know:

   1. why does she want to discontinue lithium? You may be able to allay fears or anxieties;
   2. has she always been compliant?
   3. has she had any relapses while on lithium?
   4. what form her original illness took and how many episodes she has had?
   5. what her current employment and responsibilities are;
   6. is there any suggestion of loss of insight suggestive of any relapse?

   A lithium level to check compliance is advisable.

   You will have to advise the patient about the advantages and disadvantages of stopping, including the risk of relapse which might severely compromise her personal or professional life.

   In the final analysis the patient must make her own decision and it is important to avoid disruption of the therapeutic relationship as it is necessary to preserve this in case of relapse.

b) See the patient again:

   has anything happened in the meantime?
   determine the severity of her depression;
   assess suicidal intent;
   it is likely that treatment would be required – probably antidepressants, (or even ECT);

   The patient might require admission, perhaps even as a detained patient.

   Lithium could be reintroduced (provided the patient agrees) once the acute relapse subsides, if you believe it is appropriate.

Q3

A solicitor requests that you give an opinion on his client, a 20 year old single mother of two, who has recently been caught shoplifting.

a) What would you do?

b) The girl is apparently of previously good character. Her partner walked out on her just after the second child was born six months ago.

c) She tells you she cannot sleep, is losing her appetite and has no friends. She believes she has no future and would be better off dead.

A3

a) First you must clarify from the solicitor what he requires, the nature of the report and the details of the offence.

See the girl for full history and examination and arrange that you obtain an informant's history, with emphasis on her reasons for committing the offence.

Look for evidence of:
any mental illness, medication, past psychiatric illness;
any life changes e.g. relationship difficulties;
clarify premorbid personality and forensic history;
look at any other reports.

b) It is important to determine the history of the relationship, of the break-up and of her reaction to it. Assess:
how has she coped?
the level of support from the family and other agencies;
is there any depression or alcohol or drugs abuse?

c) Her symptoms are suggestive of depressive illness. Assess the severity and nature of the depression, e.g. reactive or post natal depression and:
suicidal risk;
risk to the children.

You need to clarify who has responsibility for treatment; it may rest with another colleague in which case you would arrange that she be seen urgently and immediate admission organised if it is warranted.

Decide treatment setting. If in-patient treatment is appropriate, child care must be arranged. Day hospital care or supervision in the community by a community psychiatric nurse may be wrong given suicidal ideation.

Commence antidepressant, supportive psychotherapy.

Social services will advise on care of children and finance.

Once she has recovered, bring her children gradually into the unit to establish her confidence in caring for them.

Follow-up should involve a social worker and a community psychiatric nurse as well as a psychiatrist. Family members may also be recruited to provide support.

A referral to Relate may be an option.

The report to the solicitor should be deferred with advice that court proceedings be postponed until she is well.

Q4

A surgical colleague at your local hospital consults you confidentially. He tells you he believes he may have contracted the HIV virus and asks your advice.

a) What would you say?

b) After a few days you find he is still operating and has failed to contact you.

c) He refuses to listen to you and tells you to "mind your own business".

    What would you do now?

A4

a) First point out that while you will be as sympathetic as possible you may require to break his confidence.

Discuss with him why he thinks he has contracted the virus – even some doctors are confused over risks:
   how long has he been concerned?
   has he told anyone?
   has he taken appropriate precautions to avoid infection of patients?
   has he taken an HIV test?

Your advice would be:
   1. Stop work immediately. He should contact the General Manager and his Clinical Director; and also his defence organisation.
   2. Obtain the advice of an expert in this field.
   3. He will probably require to undergo HIV testing if he has not already done so: he should be counselled about this.
   4. You should remind him of his personal obligations and responsibilities to his family.

You should also ascertain what his mental state is and whether he requires psychiatric treatment.

b) Contact him and ascertain if he followed your advice.

You must remind him of his (and your own) obligations.

c) You must break his confidence and would have the support of the GMC in so doing.

Contact the General Manager and his Clinical Director immediately.

The surgeon should be suspended immediately on pay while appropriate investigations and arrangements are made.

Provide psychological support during this process.

Avoid being judgemental and continually re-assess the suicidal risk. You may feel the psychological support would better be provided by someone other than yourself.

Q1

You are asked to see a 34 year old lady with a history of depression which, in the past, has required hospital admission. She is married with a 2 year old son and her husband tells you that he cannot cope much longer.

a) How would you manage this case?

b) Her husband requests that he see you.

   What will you tell him?

A1

a) (As with any referral). Take a full history and examination.

Speak to her husband and another informant (if possible) as husband is exhibiting stress.

Look at old notes. If possible speak to other psychiatrists who have treated her previously.

You would wish to:
1. establish the diagnosis of depression – is it unipolar or bipolar?
how many episodes have there been?
how has she responded to treatment and has it been appropriate?
has prophylactic treatment been tried, particularly lithium?
2. rule out other mental or physical illnesses;
3. establish (if possible) precipitating and perpetuating factors, e.g. low self esteem, unemployment, poor marital relationship;
4. be wary of alcohol or drug abuse;
5. establish the husband's attitude and what his future plans are; has he any mental illness himself?
6. establish the child is not being unduly affected.

The management is:
1. prevention of illness (if possible) by increasing social support and dealing with perpetuating factors and use of medication;
2. early treatment if and when relapse occurs.
(ECT might be used at an earlier stage than normally.)

b) Find out why he wishes to see you.

Obviously it is important to gain the patient's permission to speak to her husband; this granted:
you would tell him the nature of his wife's illness, its causes and antecedents and its long term prognosis;
you should be optimistic but not unrealistically so;
you should point out that instability in home circumstances is not beneficial;
you can offer various means of support to help him cope, e.g. relatives/carers groups, day care, family support, even respite admissions;
you should advise him about the chances of his child being affected;
you should guide him but not influence him in his decision making.

Q2

A 30 year old female GP telephones you at home one night, complaining of tiredness, anxiety, low mood and irritability. She also tells you that her husband was involved in a road traffic accident, some three months previously, after a seizure.

Discuss the issues this raises for your management – ethical and otherwise.

A2

First of all clarify your position – are you being consulted casually as a friend or in a professional capacity?

If casually, you may give general advice but suggest she consult someone officially. You need do more only if you suspect her ability to do her job is in jeopardy (see below).

If you are being consulted professionally:
    arrange an interview;
    take a full history and examination;
    find out how long she has been affected;
    does she think her performance at work has suffered?
    has she taken or received any treatment?
    get a history from her own GP.

The basis for this is to:
    1. establish a diagnosis and institute a treatment plan including medication and appropriate placement;
    2. deal with perpetuating factors;
    3. decide if she is fit to continue work.
        (a) If she is fit: her performance should be closely monitored and you would need to consider seeking her permission to consult her practice colleagues.
        (b) If she is not fit: she should go on sick leave, notify her local authorities and arrange cover until she is well enough to return to work.
        (c) If she refuses to comply, or initially complies but then refuses to continue: you must consider whether she is a risk to others, especially her patients, as a result of impaired judgement.
        (d) If she is such a risk and if she continues to refuse to stop work: you are forced to contact the General Medical Council which can impose treatment on her and remove her right to practice (Refer to GMC's document "Fitness to Practice").

The other ethical issue concerns her husband:
    what were the circumstances of the accident?
    has he/she notified the Police?
    is he still driving?
    has he been investigated following the seizure?

A GP has a duty to pass relevant information to the Police. Her husband should not be driving if there is a possibility of a further seizure. You might have to tell the authorities directly and you should tell her so.

Finally, the problems relating to her husband may be the cause or part of the cause of her illness and this would be relevant in deciding upon treatment.

Q3

The parents of a 12 year old boy are sent to see you. He has recently begun to miss school and they are concerned his education may suffer.

a) What approach would you take?

b) He has missed so much time, the education authorities have visited the home. When he does attend, he behaves well and is of above average intelligence.

c) He is the youngest child, his father being a merchant naval captain. His mother suffered from post natal depression in the past.

A3

a) Arrange to see the boy and his parents for a full history and examination.

Determine whether he is refusing to go to school or is truanting and look for other changes in behaviour or mood. Also obtain details of his previous behaviour.

Enquire into the family life, parental relationship, other siblings' behaviour and any changes at school or home.

Look for evidence of physical illness or mental illness in either parents or child.

Look for criminal record or alcohol or drugs abuse in parents and child.

Obtain information from GP and teachers to corroborate history and gain insight into his behaviour and performance at school.

b) This suggests the problem may be at home. It would be important to interview parents separately. School refusal should be considered as a diagnosis.

c) This may be suggestive of illness of a depressive nature or sheer loneliness in the mother. Any illness should be treated and supportive psychotherapy given.

Insist on the need for the boy to attend school.

The mother may be keeping the boy at home for company for herself. Day Hospital attendance (for her) may be required so permitting the child to attend school.

Marital therapy could also be suggested.

Q4

a) You are asked to see urgently a 27 year old married man who has become extremely anxious and depressed recently.

b) You find that he has been having a relationship with a 43 year old man who has recently become unwell.

c) The patient's male partner has had a positive HIV test recently. The patient is afraid he too might have become infected and he asks your advice.

A4

a) First determine why the GP wishes the man seen urgently, e.g. he may consider him a suicidal risk where direct admission may be more appropriate.

Arrange to see the man for a full history and examination and obtain an informant's history from his wife.

It would be particularly important to clarify if he has a depressive illness or anxiety state.

Look for biological features:
    suicidal ideation;
    alcohol/drug abuse;
    life changes – grief or marital problems.

Any family history of mental illness or past psychiatric history would be relevant.

b) Clarify whether the relationship is sexual and whether his friend is, or suspects he may be, HIV positive. Determine if he is in (any) other risk group(s), e.g. intravenous drug user.

This suggests the man is concerned about the risk to himself of AIDS/HIV. The subject should be discussed in detail and he should be advised to have an HIV test with associated counselling. Advice should also be offered concerning his general sexual practices and the question of the patient discussing the matter with his wife should be broached.

c) You should continue to advise HIV testing. He must avoid sexual contact with others until he is certain he will not pass on the virus. He should be strongly advised to discuss the matter with his wife. Appropriate psychological support should be provided for both.

Any co-incidental illness should be treated, e.g. anxiety management and relaxation therapy; antidepressants; supportive psychotherapy.

Q1

a) You are asked to see a 27 year old young woman with Down's Syndrome who lives with her elderly parents. Over the past few months she has become increasingly difficult to manage. She will not rise or go to bed until it suits her, she is moody and has been physically violent as well.

b) There have been several episodes of disturbed behaviour when she has been incontinent of urine.

c) In the end, the parents state they cannot cope any more with her at home.

A1

a) Obtain from GP, and any hospital, details or notes of this girl's physical, mental and behavioural history as well as present medication.

Arrange to see the young woman and her parents and obtain a full history and examination. Note her behaviour with the parents. Find out if her behaviour varies in different environments:

clarify the change in behaviour and look for changes in surroundings and medication;

clarify parents' concern – especially support, future placement;

look for physical or mental illness;

assess level of input from primary health care and social services;

consider possibility of abuse.

If illness is present, commence treatment:

if it is a behavioural problem it will require behaviour regimen;

possible increase in day centre care, holiday respite and financial support;

change in medication may be considered.

b) This may suggest a seizure; has she a history or is this a new presentation?

Alternatively it may be due to mental illness, a physical illness (e.g. an UTI) or behavioural.

Arrange appropriate investigations to see if she is an undiagnosed epileptic.

Check her compliance with medication; also check her:
MSSU;   blood sugar;   full blood count.

If required: commence or alter anticonvulsant medication.

Even if an epileptic, pseudoseizures are still possible.

c) Discuss the various long term options for placement.

Involvement of a social worker for the mentally handicapped is invaluable. As a result of recent legislation, a multidisciplinary assessment may be required so as to allow the care manager to use his/her funds most appropriately; options include:

remain at home with increased support and/or respite;

hospital admission;

nursing home, hostel or group home;

independent living with or without support.

Q2

A 27 year old married man is referred to you. For some time he has been aware of feeling anxious most of the time, he is becoming reluctant to leave the house and is afraid he is mentally ill.

a) How would you deal with this?

b) On review he appears to have had several distinct panic attacks when out, resulting in an immediate return home. Now he is refusing to leave the house at all and his wife is thinking of giving up her job.

c) His sleep pattern is very poor, he is getting upset and complains that he is getting depressed.

A2

a) Arrange to see this young man for a full history and examination; a domiciliary visit may be required.

Clarify the nature of the anxiety symptoms, especially onset and precipitants; consider agoraphobia or panic attacks.

Look for:
    depressive illness;
    alcohol and drugs abuse;
    is there delusional basis for anxiety?

Obtain an informant's history.

b) The information provided suggests panic attacks and possibly agoraphobia. However other disorders, e.g. depression, may be present (which may require treatment).

The treatment regimen, in panic/agoraphobia, would involve a behavioural approach.
    Treat associated problems e.g. depression by:
    1. cognitive and supportive psychotherapy;
    2. anxiety management;
    3. relaxation;
    4. medication, e.g. SSRIs/imipramine, may be effective.

A community psychiatric nurse could deliver treatment and then organise attendance at a day hospital.

Advise wife not to give up job. This is likely to make husband worse. She herself may require support.

c) Clearly depression must be considered.

Reassure the patient that treatment is available.

If antidepressants have not been used they could be introduced if indicated.

Beware of perpetuating factors: marital problems, alcohol abuse etc.

Q3

You are asked to see a 46 year old woman by her GP. Six years ago she had an episode of depression. Recently, the family have noted that she has become disinhibited in her behaviour and has been putting objects in her mouth.

a) How would you deal with this?

b) What investigations would you carry out?

c) What familial disorder would you have in mind?

A3

a) Visit the woman at home in the presence of a family member.

First of all take a full history. Perform an examination and a detailed cognitive assessment. Speak to an informant.

The history is suggestive of a personality change with frontal lobe components. Look for other aspects of a frontal lobe lesion, e.g.:
irritability;
reduced impulse control;
labile emotions;
apathetic attitude or evidence of a Kluver-Bucy like syndrome (visual agnosia, hypersexuality, hyperphagia, compulsive oral and handling behaviour).

Are there any other neurological signs affecting, for example, speech or motor neurones?

You need to rule out trauma.

Take an alcohol/drug history.

Is there a family history?

Is the patient aware of what she is doing?

What are the supports like and can she remain at home?

b) The main investigation would be a CT scan as well as an EEG.

A CT scan might show atrophy, particularly in frontal and temporal regions and might help rule out a neoplasm.

c) The likely diagnosis is Pick's disease: which is autosomal dominant in a large number of cases. The usual age of onset is 50-60. The course is slower than presenile Alzheimer's disease. Counselling of relatives is required in view of the chronic personality change. Behavioural management may work in the early stages. Thioridazine is also of some benefit.

Consider day care/day hospital. Liaise with Social Services. Offer respite. Benzodiazepines should be avoided as they make disinhibition worse. Eventually institutional care is likely to be required.

Q4

A 62 year old woman is attending your day hospital with a history of depression. She arrives at the hospital one morning heavily made up and discussing her personal life at the top of her voice.

a) What would you do?

b) She is presently on antidepressants and you are reviewing her management.

   What would you do?

A4

a) First clarify whose patient this woman is.

This is suggestive of a hypomanic phase. If she is under treatment with a colleague you should inform him/her as to what you observed.

If she is under your care;
> you need to see her to check her history and carry out a mental state examination and speak to an informant; (examination of her medical notes would reveal whether there have been previous hypomanic episodes and, if so, their duration and response to treatment); ascertain if there have been any recent life events.
> find out about sleep pattern, appetite and libido;
> has she been taking her medication?
> rule out drug/alcohol abuse;
> have a physical examination or investigations carried out if you suspect a physical illness.

b) In the event that it is a hypomanic phase with no other complicating factors:
> the antidepressants may be a factor (especially if a tricyclic), they should be withdrawn slowly;
> neuroleptic medication should be introduced and increased to a therapeutic level;
> admission may be advisable and much depends on the level of insight and degree of home support;
> if there is a substantial risk of physical harm to herself or others, compulsory admission may be required.

Once she is recovering, lithium prophylaxis should be introduced (if she is not already on it), provided she consents and there is no contra-indication.

She should be monitored closely on discharge for depressive phases which should be treated carefully and perhaps with a newer S.S.R.I. drug.

Q1

A GP in a small town rings you up. He tells you that a patient of his, a 34 year old single woman who lives in a remote farm with her father, has been writing unsolicited love letters to several members of the local Police force.

a) He asks for your advice.

b) He asks you do a home visit but her father is hostile and refuses to let you see his daughter. Your impression is that the farm house is in a state of squalor.

c) Eventually you meet the daughter who appears to be of low IQ and ill-cared for. A local social worker has also expressed concern.

   What advice would you give?

A1

a) Determine the details of the letters, enquire as to the woman's past mental health, whether there is any mental handicap, physical illness, alcohol abuse or mental illness.

Also obtain as much information on the father and family as possible.

Suggest you would be happy to see her if required, a domiciliary visit may be the most informative.

Causes could be:
low IQ;
personality;
psychotic illness, e.g. schizophrenia; De Clerambault's syndrome.

b) This would lead you to believe that the level of functioning may be impaired in either or both individuals.

It is important to obtain as much information as possible on past mental state and functioning.

Tell the social services of your concern about the squalor and your concern for this woman. They may be able to gain access.

c) Advise full physical examination and history to look for any physical or mental illness (including psychometric assessment to ascertain IQ) – if present they require treatment.

It may be that she is not ill but rather neglected. The father may have a treatable mental or physical illness which when dealt with would permit him to care for his daughter with appropriate support from the social services.

If he is not ill or refuses treatment or support you would need to consider the wellbeing of the girl.

A guardianship order might be required.

The girl, if mentally handicapped, might benefit from placement in a mental handicap hostel and attendance at a day centre or sheltered workshop.

You should discuss this with local social services.

Q2

You are asked to see a 19 year old girl who has attended your local Accident and Emergency (A&E) Department. She has just attempted to slash her wrists and says she will do it again.

a) How would you proceed with this case?

b) You find that the wounds are superficial. In addition, she has made numerous attempts in the past to cut her wrists and throat.

   Would this affect your management?

c) She becomes abusive and tells you everyone hates her and that if you do not admit her she will kill herself.

   What would you do?

A2

(a) See this girl for a full history and examination, with the following questions in your mind:

why did she do it?

was there a precipitant, e.g. family row, lovers tiff?

where and when she did it;

did she write a note and did she attempt to avoid detection?

was it planned or impulsive?

what did she do afterwards, (e.g. did she self-refer to A&E)?

does she regets her actions?

was alcohol involved?

Carry out a mental state examination – looking for mental illness, suicidal ideation.

Obtain an informant's history, GP and hospital notes (if possible).

If she is a suicidal risk, admit her; if she refuses, consider detention.

If she is not a suicidal risk but is mentally ill, treat and arrange appropriate follow-up:

treatment would be determined by the severity of the illness, level of community and family support etc.;

if she requires follow-up, consider by whom (social workers or GP?)

If there is no evidence of mental illness, advise her concerning her behaviour and consider if follow-up required.

b) [There is an increased risk of suicide in those with deliberate self harm (one hundred-fold).] Has she been assessed before? Is something being overlooked?

Look for:

sexual abuse/family problems;

drugs/alcohol abuse;

personality difficulties.

It is important not to react with hostility.

c) She is unhappy and is using self harm as a threat. You need to be sure you are not missing a mental illness. If her judgement is not impaired by mental illness, she is responsible for her own actions and should be told so. Nonetheless she may benefit from follow-up by a sympathetic Mental Health Worker. Gradually she may learn to use other methods to alleviate her distress and obtain help in a constructive way.

Q3

A GP refers a 35 year old single woman to you. She has a long history of migraine. Over the last 6 months she has vomited frequently, even without headaches. The GP is worried that she has an eating disorder.

a) How would you deal with this?

b) You discover she had problems with nausea and abdominal pain as a child and failed to sit her A levels due to headaches.

    How would you treat her?

A3

a) First of all ensure that a complete physical examination and appropriate investigations have been carried out.

Then see the patient herself, take a full history and examine her, speak to an informant (if possible).

The GP is worried about an eating disorder. Is there any evidence for this, e.g.:
  marked weight loss;
  abnormal attitudes to food and weight;
  menstrual irregularities;
  bulimia and use of laxatives;
  excessive exercise?

If there is little to support an eating disorder, other possibilities are:
  anxiety disorder;
  depression;
  hysterical illness;
  malingering;
  unsuspected physical illness.

The differential diagnosis would be clarified by the history and mental state examination.

b) This evidence is supportive of an anxiety neurosis – she appears to have had anxiety/neurotic problems for some years.

Try to identify why it has become worse, looking at:
  social outlets;
  job;
  family and personal relationships;
  are there any stresses?
  is there any underlying depression?

Treat any depressive element appropriately.

Anxiety can be treated by education, relaxation techniques and self monitoring to demonstrate success.

In some cases use of an antidepressant may help; benzodiazepines should be avoided.

The patient should not become too reliant on the therapist!

Self-reliance needs to be fostered.

Q4

A community psychiatric nurse contacts you about a 60 year old bachelor found wandering in the fields by his sister. He is receiving a depot injection which was omitted 2 weeks ago because he was bedridden with a back problem.

a) What will you do?

His diagnosis is chronic schizophrenia. He refuses to attend your out-patient clinic and in the past has ignored all appointments.

b) What action would you take?

A4

a) If you are not acquainted with his history peruse his old notes. Speak to his GP. Get further information from his community psychiatric nurse.

Next you need to see the patient – preferably at home and speak to his sister. Make a mental state examination and a physical examination to rule out any physical illness; asking yourself especially:

how long has he been ill?
what is his diagnosis?
how frequently he relapses?
what his normal behaviour is like?
is he suffering from paranoid ideation, delusions or hallucinations?
is he confused?
is he confabulating?

Possible diagnoses are:

1. relapse of schizophrenia;
2. onset of dementing illness;
3. acute confusional state;
4. substance intoxication or withdrawal or sequelae;
5. other physcial illness.

Treatment involves:

1. medication – treat any acute illness and consider whether or not to continue with depot;
2. decide if he requires admission or not for investigation and/or treatment;
3. consider long term placement – he could remain at home plus increased support and/or day centre or go to a hostel/nursing home;
4. arrange follow up – either at an out-patient clinic or by a community psychiatric nurse.

b) In this situation you cannot force him to attend an out-patient clinic:

would he consider day hospital or day centre?
would he permit his GP to follow up at his surgery?
would he allow a community psychiatric nurse to call regularly and liaise with you?

His sister could be recruited to monitor his condition and make contact at suggestion of deterioration which might be prevented by increasing medication. If a relapse was severe, admission would be an option, either voluntarily or involuntarily.

Q1

A 19 year old young man was admitted to an inpatient unit. He was aggressive and experiencing paranoid delusions. He was treated with chlorpromazine but 48 hours later developed a fever of 39.6°c.

a) How would you proceed?

b) If a diagnosis of Neuroleptic Malignant Syndrome were made, how would you manage him in the future?

A1

a) Take a full history and examine him thoroughly. Ask about previous exposure to neuroleptics. Look for evidence of common causes of pyrexia, e.g. URTI

It is important to rule out:

1. neuroleptic malignant syndrome (NMS: automonic instability, fluctuating pulse and blood pressure, rigidity, confusion);
2. neuroleptic induced agranulocytosis (NIA);
3. intracranial disease e.g. encephalitis, meningitis, abscess.

Check: FBP;   WCC;   creatinine kinase;
       chest x-ray;   lumbar puncture;   CT scan.

If there is a likely infective cause – institute the appropriate treatment and continually review progress.

If there are features of NMS – stop all neuroleptics immediately; use appropriate supportive treatment, (dantrolene and/or bromocriptine may be used). He should be referred to a medical unit.

The mental state may require use of non-neuroleptics e.g. paraldehyde (benzodiazepines may produce paradoxical aggression).

If there are features of NIA, stop medication and refer to medical unit.

If there is an intracranial disease – refer to a neurologist.

b) 1. Pharmacological treatment.
Neuroleptics would not be ruled out. Much depends on the balance between the effects of his psychosis versus the risk of a further episode of NMS. There is theoretical evidence to suggest that thioridazine is less likely to cause NMS than chlorpromazine or haloperidol. Other authorities recommend clozapine but there are risks in this as well.

A neuroleptic could be re-introduced carefully and slowly with suitable gradual increases in dosage. Injectable forms should be avoided, if possible. The patient, his relatives and GP should be aware of the NMS.

2. Non-pharmacological treatment.
He will require close and careful community follow-up to try to spot relapses early. He should carry a warning card and, ideally, an identity bracelet.

Try to have experienced staff involved when admitted.

Q2

A 30 year old single teacher is referred to you by her GP who is unsure about management. She has been despondent and unhappy for two years.

a) What would you suggest?

She lived with her parents until she was 29. Since then she has bought her first home and has changed her job to one with increased responsibility.

b) What would you do?

A2

a) Obtain a full history and examination. Find out what treatment she has been given and its duration, whether she took it and how she responded.

   The history of this woman appears to point to a depressive illness. If this is the case:
   try to assess how long she has been ill;
   clarify if she has been continually ill or if there has been fluctuation in her mood and determine the severity of her depression (biological features and degree of dysfunction);
   what are the likely precipitants?
   are there any perpetuating factors?
   what are her supports like?
   consider substance abuse, personality disorder or the presence of another psychiatric illness.

b) She may be having problems adjusting to these changes:
   why did she leave home (at the time she did)?
   does she live alone or have a close friend or partner?
   how is she coping with her new job?
   is she having financial difficulties?
   is there a suicidal risk?

   Treatment would be:
   1. identify causal or perpetuating factors over a period of time in a supportive psychotherapeutic relationship – these could be looked at with a view to development of coping strategies;
   2. advise regarding any substance abuse;
   3. if there is a relationship problem: consider referral or advice on this;
   4. she may benefit from referral to a sympathetic financial adviser;
   5. consider antidepressant treatment;
   6. consider prophylaxis, especially if previous episode of bipolar illness.

   NB (If there is a risk of suicide then this needs immediate consideration. Admission may well be necessary – even against her wishes).

Q3

During one of your clinics you hear a commotion outside. You find that one of the patients, a 45 year old man, has collapsed and appears to be fitting.

a) What would you do?

b) It transpires that he has never had a seizure before. He has a past history of schizophrenia but is well controlled on a small depot injection.

c) An EEG shows no evidence of a mass lesion or epileptic activity. A CT Scan also is, apparently, normal.

d) Two weeks later, the patient's employers write to you and ask if he is still able to carry out his job gardening in the local park.

A3

a) Ask the staff to clear the area so that you can deal with the patient and ask them to bring the emergency kit (drugs and airways etc.) and treat as an emergency:

    1. roll the patient onto his side, clear his airway, ensure he is breathing. Confirm he is fitting. Smell his breath for alcohol or ketones;

    2. administer an intravenous benzodiazepine. If not possible administer diazepam PR. Remove to private situation when seizure ceases;

    3. attempt to identify patient – personal effects, identity bracelet, especially note if epileptic or diabetic;

    4. look for signs of head injury or other trauma sustained by fall and fit;

    5. have him observed until he is fully recovered.

b) Neuroleptics lower the fitting threshold but this man will require admission for full investigation to determine the cause.

Carry out a full history and examination. Note increases or changes in medication, alcohol or other drugs, family history or head injury.

c) In time a cause may become apparent.

If no cause is evident his depot medication should be stopped if possible, and if medication is still required an oral form should be given.

Keep under regular review by community psychiatric nurse or at out-patient clinic.

Make sure his GP is informed.

d) Inform employer that the patient's details can be released only with his permission. When obtained tell them that he is permitted to hold a licence if he has no fits for two years or only night time fits for three years. They will have to assess the risks to him in his work situation. The patient should have the opportunity to discuss his concerns with the doctor.

Q4

You are asked to see a middle-aged housewife who gives a long history of anxiety, panic attacks and depression. Many years ago, her former GP prescribed diazepam and she has been taking it ever since.

a) How would you proceed?

b) She appears to be physically addicted to her diazepam and is afraid you will stop it on her.

Despite a very gradual withdrawal, she remains anxious and panicky and says she cannot cope.

c) What would you do?

A4

a) Clarify why you are seeing this woman: to treat her depression and/or anxiety, or for withdrawal from benzodiazepines?

Arrange to see her for full history and examination.

Obtain an informant's history from her husband and a detailed history from her GP of the course of her illness and medications prescribed; does he suspect drugs or alcohol abuse?

Has she been seen before? If so obtain notes.

If no mental illness is present, provide detoxification regimen and supportive psychotherapy.

If there is mental illness, treat her for depression, anxiety or panic disorder. This may be followed by the detoxification regimen. Given the duration, day hospital or in-patient treatment may be necessary, including:
    antidepressants;   anxiety management;
    relaxation therapy;   group or individual psychotherapy.

It is important not to miss a physical illness.

b) There will also be a strong psychological addiction. She will need to discuss her fears. Discuss the detoxification regimen and the aim of stopping the use of benzodiazepines. Provide treatment for any anxiety disorder or depression by means without addictive consequences. Explain the physical symptoms and expected duration.

c) Repeat examination and history.

Check any possibility of a missed diagnosis (e.g. panic disorder, depression, alcohol abuse, physical disease) or of (non)compliance.

Beware of any life events or other factors which have prevented recovery.

Treat any disorder appropriately:
    if depression – consider alternative treatment, e.g. SSRIs;
    if panic disorder – may need additional support from community psychiatric nurse.

Look out for:
    still obtaining diazepam;   substitution by other drugs;
    alcohol problems;   physical illness;
    marital problems.

PAPER XII

Q1

You are asked to see a 42 year old small businessman who stopped his lithium six months ago. He has become irritable and difficult to cope with. His wife, who works as his secretary, says he has insulted some of his customers.

a) What would you do?

b) The patient refuses to be admitted and insists you leave his home.

c) The man eventually is admitted as a detained patient.

   How would you manage him?

A1

a) Obtain the maximum information from his wife, GP and hospital notes; look especially for:

> previous diagnosis, e.g. manic depressive psychosis;
> why he came off his treatment, e.g. side effects?
> whether on other medication, e.g. neuroleptics?
> pattern of illness and behaviour in past.

Arrange to see him for full history and examination with special emphasis on mental state examination, looking for mood changes and any delusions.

Gain a clear picture of present behaviour, e.g. threatening violence or self harm.

Determine diagnosis and setting for treatment.

Most likely diagnosis is hypomania.

Commence neuroleptics. Treatment options are:

> 1. community supervision by Community Psychiatric Nurse and GP;
> 2. day hospital;
> 3. in-patient – in view of his business problems this would be the best option.

b) The patient has the right to ask you to leave. If you believe that he is a risk to others or himself by virtue of mental illness you should advise detention. If not, inform his GP and wife of situation and advise on appropriate medication.

c) Observe his mental state and behaviour to confirm his diagnosis. If you suspect drug or alcohol abuse screen his urine and check his liver function. Manage agitation with experienced staff plus medication (neuroleptics).

Treat hypomania with neuroleptics. Lithium may be added if required.

Any subsequent depressive episodes can be treated with antidepressants plus neuroleptics if psychotic or agitated.

Relaxation therapy and supportive therapy will be beneficial when he is more settled.

Look for precipitants, e.g. pressure of business, quality of marriage, alcohol abuse.

He will need careful follow-up and would benefit from long term prophylaxis with lithium.

Q2

A GP requests that you visit a 72 year old man who lives alone, his wife having recently died. Neighbours say he has been behaving oddly and is wandering at night.

a) How would you manage this case?

The GP tells you he is on salbutamol, frusemide, amitriptyline, cimetidine and amoxycillin. The old man at interview appears confused.

b) What would you advise?

c) You feel sure the man is quite demented, he has no relatives and appears to be unable to return home.

A2

a) First clarify from the GP what he found when he saw the man. If he has not seen and examined the man, ask him to do so.

An acute organic state must be ruled out and treatment given if appropriate.

If it is necessary for you to see the man, take a full history and examination, if possible in his home, and obtain an informant's history. Special emphasis should be placed on organic mental state and affective state.

Determine details of his mood and behaviour prior to his wife's death and whether she was the main carer. Try to obtain details of any medication or changes in medication.

b) Assess whether the man is suffering from an acute confusional state. Likely causes would be:
  1. chest infection or other infection;
  2. heart failure;
  3. medication e.g. amitriptyline or cimetidine;
  4. electrolyte disturbance;
  5. myocardial infarction;
  6. CVA;
  7. alcohol intoxication.

Refer the patient for investigation and treatment of physical illness, having discussed this with his GP. Discontinue any unnecessary medication, e.g. if not depressed, stop amitriptyline.

Consider ECG, chest x-ray, bloods for sugar, LFT's, U&E, full blood count.

When the acute confusional state is treated, you must rule out an underlying chronic brain syndrome.

There are suggestions of a dementing process in the history, e.g. the wandering. His wife may have covered up for his deficiencies.

c) In this case you need to liaise with his GP and tell him of your findings. Admission to a psychogeriatric unit for further assessment might be appropriate, if he is not already in one. If he was judged suitable for community placement, his local care manager should be contacted so as to co-ordinate the various services.

Q3

A 14 year old girl is on holiday with relatives. She takes an overdose and you are asked to see her in the medical ward.

a) What would you do?

Three years ago her mother died. She lives alone with her father and tells you how unhappy she has been since then. Her father is arriving from another part of the country.

b) What would you do?

A3

a) See her once she has fully recovered from her overdose.

As with any case you require full history and examination. It would be beneficial to speak to ward staff and find out about mood, sleep, appetite and interaction. Her relatives may also be able to give useful information.

You need to determine:
   her reasons for the overdose;
   what she took;
   why she took it;
   any plans she may have made and her attitude now;
   have there been previous attempts?

It is important to determine:
   1. if there is a treatable underlying illness – depression in adolescents is often missed;
   2. the extent of suicidal intent and the risk of future attempts;
   3. try to find the cause.

In all girls of this age, a psychosexual history is important.

You may require several visits to gain her confidence. The help of a sympathetic hospital social worker or nurse may be invaluable.

You want to know:
   is there any suggestion of sexual and/or physical abuse?
   is she sexually active and might she be pregnant?
   may there be substance abuse?

b) Her father will obviously be anxious to find out what has happened. He may be able to give invaluable background information. You should be wary of betraying confidences to him.

You plan would be:
   1. arrange treatment of any mental illness;
   2. counsel her initially regarding the risks of deliberate self harm;
   3. try to find the cause;
   4. arrange the appropriate follow-up in her locality;
   5. substance abuse may need to be addressed.

If there has been sexual abuse you would need to notify the local social services department of your concerns.

Q4

You are asked to see a 17 year old man who was brought to your local hospital. He had been caught smashing windows, was acting strangely and out of character.

a) What would you do?

b) There was no smell of alcohol but he admitted taking illicit drugs in the last two weeks.

He refused to stay in hospital although his parents insisted that he do so.

c) What would you do?

A4

a) Ascertain who has made the request and why.

Assuming it is the A&E Officer who was worried about an underlying psychiatric illness, you would proceed as follows:
obtain a full history and mental state examination with emphasis on what he had been doing, for how long and did he know why?
interview a relative or witness (if possible);
get account from A&E Staff as to what they observed.

You need to decide if he is mentally ill or not.

If he is mentally ill – what is the diagnosis?
Possibilities include drugs/alcohol leading to intoxication or withdrawal, an organic cause (e.g. epilepsy) or a coincidential mental illness.

If not mentally ill – he no longer requires psychiatric input.

b) You will need a fuller drug history.
What drugs he took, when and for how long?
What were the usual effects?
Look for evidence of dependence.

Remember drug experimentation is common and may not be causal.

Decide if he needs in-patient or out-patient care.

c) You need to decide if he requires detention for assessment. In this case, you must suspect a substantial risk of physical harm to himself or others and that he is suffering from a mental disorder. If he warrants detention, arrange for him to be detained in the A&E Department and then transferred to his local psychiatric unit using the appropriate forms.

The implications of intravenous usage and its consequences should be addressed (e.g. HIV) even if there is no obvious dependence. Consider referral to support groups.

If he does not require detention, give appropriate advice and arrange follow-up.

A4

a) In this case it is important to determine the reason for referral e.g. whether alcohol is the only reason.

Carry out a full history and examination – look for:
    alcohol dependence (or other drugs);
    mental illness (e.g. depression);
    physical illness.

An informant's history is particularly important as the patient may be less than honest. Psychiatric hospital or other medical notes should be obtained.

If alcohol dependence is diagnosed, discuss the need for abstinence and explain the unrealistic aim of controlled drinking:
    1. determine need for detoxification – at home (GP) if low risk, in hospital if high risk (poor physical condition, epilespy);
    2. refer to education and support groups – patient and family (AA, Al-Anon);
    3. treat physical illness – refer as appropriate;
    4. treat psychiatric illness – important to re-assess as withdrawal completed; assess suicidal risk and avoid addictive medication.

(b) If the diagnosis remained undetected at initial interview see again. Ask him to bring his wife. Re-assess mental state; look for:
    normal jealousy;
    pathological jealousy;
    any mental illness;
    assess dangerousness, e.g. history of violence, threats, plans.

c) Contact the GP urgently and the man's wife and inform them of the risks. The wife should be advised to seek sanctuary in the interim.

Further management depends on the diagnosis.

A period of assessment in a mental hospital would be helpful: there appear to be adequate grounds for detention if required.

In the absence of mental illness or a reason for admission the matter becomes the responsibility of the civil authorities.